# Rail Fence Quilt

## For Kids at Heart

LuAnn Stout

*To my husband, Jay, and my two children, Tom and Nancy, for their complete support, encouragement, and confidence in my abilities. Thank you for being my best fans.*

Published by Quilt in a Day®, Inc.

1955 Diamond Street, San Marcos, CA 92069

Copyright © 1993 by LuAnn Stout

First Printing  September 1993


ISBN  0-922705-44-5

Editor  Eleanor Burns

Art Direction  Merritt Voigtlander

# Table of Contents

# Introduction

As a young girl I spent many happy hours on our farm in southeastern Idaho. There was work that had to be done, but we always had time to dream, imagine, and play.

Like most farms we also had sheep, cows, horses, and chickens. So it was necessary to have "fenced corrals" for the animals. Ours were wooden rail fences. It was great fun to see how far you could walk along the top rail without falling off. This was my imaginary highway that I walked to far away countries and the big cities. These fences were easy to climb, fun to walk, and perfect for sitting to watch the animals.

Some of my favorite times were sitting on the rail fence watching my father feed the sheep. I would talk with him as he carried the grain to the feeders and spread the hay in mounds around the corral.

I dedcided Rail Fence would be a perfect beginner's quilt book. I wrote it with short, clear directions and put in pictures to show the ideas. The center rail was made wide to help keep the block straight and make the quilt easy and very fast.

This book is written for kids of all ages. It can be used as a text for children, juniors, or first time quilters.

Directions are given for tearing the fabric and cutting with scissors because using a rotary cutter by a child or someone not familiar with it can be dangerous.

I hope the Rail Fence quilt will give you many happy hours and memories of quilting, just as writing this book for you has given me the pleasure of remembering the rail fences of my childhood.

# Annie's Trip to the Farm

Annie yawned, stretched, and opened her eyes. She looked around. Where was she? The wall paper with pink roses and the lace curtains gently blowing at the window did not look familiar. Then she remembered, she was at her Grandparents' house on the farm.

It was Annie's first trip to the farm without the rest of her family and she had been excited to come. She worried a little that she might get homesick, but this was her third day here, and she was too busy to miss home.

There was always lots of work to do. Annie's jobs, though, were more fun than work. Why just yesterday Granny let her feed wheat to the chickens, put water in the little troughs, and gave her a basket to gather the eggs. It was noisy in the chicken coop, but it was such fun to watch the chickens scratch around in the straw, peck at the food, and cluck to each other! Annie remembered the rooster with his big tail feathers strutting around the chicken coop as if to say, "Look at me. I am beautiful."

She snuggled under the warm quilts and listened to the sounds of the farm. She could hear Granny rattling the dishes as she fixed breakfast in the kitchen downstairs. The birds were chirping their cheery songs and somewhere in the distance a dog was barking. It seemed to Annie at this very moment that everything was perfect.

Just then Granny called, "Breakfast, Annie."

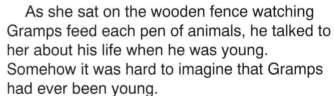

Annie helped Granny all morning in the house dusting and tidying up and then in the garden weeding. After the lunch dishes were done, she went to the barnyard where she loved to see the animals. She sat with Gramps on the wooden fence that he had built and watched the mother sheep with their little lambs. One mother sheep stamped her foot at Annie.

"She doesn't want you looking at her lamb," said Gramps. "That is her way of saying 'Go away'."

Annie loved the little lambs. They were so playful. Gramps jumped into the corral and picked up one lamb he called "a bum lamb."

"The mother died and this lamb will die if it isn't given milk," he told her. From then on each night Annie fed the "bum lamb" milk from an oversize baby bottle.

About sundown each day Gramps would call from the porch, "Annie would you like to go with me to do the evening chores?" Chores really meant caring for the animals and seeing that all on the farm were bedded down for the night.

Evening was her favorite time of the day. The air was still and smelled of hay. The animals were quiet, and it made Annie feel warm and quiet, too.

As she sat on the wooden fence watching Gramps feed each pen of animals, he talked to her about his life when he was young. Somehow it was hard to imagine that Gramps had ever been young.

"Do you know what they call that wooden fence where you are sitting?" asked Gramps as he closed the corral gate and picked up the empty feed buckets.

"Does it have a name?" Annie replied with surprise.

"Indeed it does. It is called the Rail Fence. There is also a song about the Rail fence called Leaning On The Old Top Rail."

"Oh, sing it for me Gramps, please, please."

Gramps laughed, "I'm not much of a singer, but you asked for it." He set down the buckets, leaned on the rail fence and sang the song. Annie was surprised how well he could sing. She cheered and clapped her hands when he finished. She was going to miss the farm when she went home.

After supper and chores the next evening Annie sat in the living room by her grandmother's side watching her sew. She picked up the large, wicker, sewing basket. "I like this basket, Granny. Is it old?"

"Oh my dear, that was my mother's—your great Grandmother! She had her sewing tools in it and always set it beside her as she mended or patched. Now I use it for my sewing. Let me show it to you."

Granny opened the basket. It was full of wonderful pieces of colored fabrics. There were plaids, stripes, and flowered pieces of all sizes and shapes. As Granny took out the pieces, she told how Annie's mother would help her cut the pieces or "scraps" into squares and patch them together. Each piece had some special meaning.

"From these patches your mother and I made beautiful quilts," said Granny.

"Do you have any of these quilts my Mother made?" asked Annie.

Laughing, Granny replied, "Look on your bed and you will see." Then Granny's eyes twinkled. "Annie, you'd like to take something home from the farm, wouldn't you? Pick out some scraps from the sewing basket and I will help you cut and stitch them into a Rail Fence Quilt."

In the following days, each evening after "chores" Annie and Granny would sew together. It was a special time when they talked about the farm, Granny's childhood and Annie's life in the city. Gramps would listen and occasionally add some story that made them all laugh. Annie loved working with the scraps and being together with both Grandparents. Soon she would be going home, but she would have a Rail Fence quilt to remind her of her visit to the farm and the happy times she'd had there.

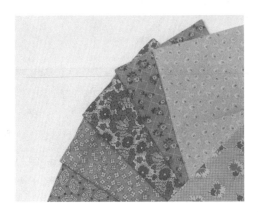

# Choosing your Rail Fence Fabrics

## Let's make a quilt.
### But how and where do we begin?

Rail Fence is a favorite beginning quilt. The middle rail is wide to keep the pattern simple. This also helps to keep the strips or rails straight.

When you choose your fabric for the wide 2nd rail, it might be a Picture Fabric. A Picture Fabric has pictures that go the same way.

This book will tell you about Picture Fabric and how much fabric you need so the pictures all go the same way. Look on pages 12,13, &14 at the Yardage and Tearing Charts that say "for using Picture Fabric." These charts tell you how much fabric you need and how to tear your strips.

If your fabric is not Picture Fabric, use the yardage chart at the top of the page. Make a quilt. You'll like it and have fun.

# Start with 3 different fabrics.

1. To begin, choose a fabric you like for your wide 2nd rail. Choose two more fabrics that look good with it. These will be 1st Rail and 3rd Rail.

2. The 1st Rail and 3rd Rail fabrics will be the rail design. The **colors** should be very different from each other.

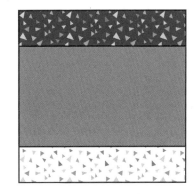

1st Rail

Wide 2nd Rail

3rd Rail

3. Think of your fabrics as light, medium or dark. These are called Different Values.

Light          Medium          Dark

4. Choose different size prints and solid fabrics for interest. These are called Different Textures.   A large print fabric will appear busy; a small print will not stand out as much and may look solid from a distance. A solid fabric can be used so the quilt will not appear too busy.

Solid          Large print

5. Fabrics should be good quality, 100% cotton.  This is important so your strips will tear straight.  Because this is "strip quilting," the fabrics must be at least 42" from selvage to selvage. Measure each fabric to be sure.

Small print          Picture fabric

Have fun with colors, values, and textures!

# Choosing Picture Fabric for the Wide 2nd Rail

Some fabrics are printed with flowers, animals or pictures all going the same way. This is called "one way" or "picture" fabric.

When the picture fabric is turned, the picture will be on its side, or upside down.

If you choose picture fabric for the wide 2nd rail, some of the picture blocks will be turned on their side.

All of your picture blocks can be straight if you tear the fabric two different ways.

If you decide to use picture fabric, be sure to use the Picture Tearing Chart on pages 12, 13 or 14.

# The Batting and the Backing

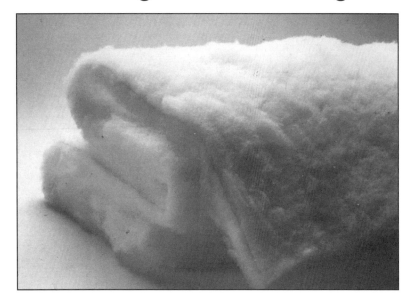

### Batting in your Quilt
Batting looks something like fluffy cotton. It is put inside of your quilt to make it either fat or thin. If you want it to be puffy, then use a thick fluffy batting. It will be warm and cozy. If you use a thin batting your quilt will look flat. When you tie a quilt, thick batting usually looks better. Be sure that you buy a batting that is called bonded batting. This is a batting that will not pull apart if you were to give it a gentle pull.

### Back of the Quilt
The back of the quilt is called backing. It can be printed or plain fabric or even a bed sheet. A printed fabric does not show dirt as much as plain fabric. If the fabric is not wide enough for your quilt, you must sew two pieces of fabric together. The sheet will be wide enough without sewing.

Choose a quilt backing that you like and will feel good against your skin.

1st Rail

Wide 2nd Rail

3rd Rail

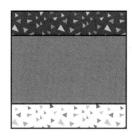

# Paste-Up Sheet

Cut out a piece of fabric from each of your rails and paste on the large block.

1st Rail

Wide 2nd Rail

3rd Rail

# Square Quilt

16 Blocks   4 across by 4 down
Finished size approx. 44" x 44" with border

## Square Size

|  | Yardage to buy |  | Tear Strips selvage to selvage |  |
|---|---|---|---|---|
| Rail 1 and 3 | ½ yd. each |  | 4 strips   2 ½" wide |  |
| Wide 2nd Rail | 1 yd. |  | 4 strips   6" wide |  |
| Border | ⅔ yd. |  | 5 strips   3" wide |  |
|  |  |  |  |  |
| Batting | 45" x 45" |  |  |  |
| Backing | 1 ½ yds. |  |  |  |

## Square Size for using Picture Fabric

|  | Yardage to buy |  | Tear Strips |  |
|---|---|---|---|---|
| Rail 1 and 3 | ½ yd. each |  | 4 strips   2 ½" wide selvage to selvage |  |
| Wide 2nd Rail | 1 ⅔ yds. |  | 2 strips   6" wide selvage to selvage |  |
|  |  |  | and 2 strips   6" wide ALONG THE SELVAGE |  |
| Border | ⅔ yd. |  | 5 strips   3" wide selvage to selvage |  |
|  |  |  |  |  |
| Batting | 45" x 45" |  |  |  |
| Backing | 1 ½ yds. |  |  |  |

# TV Quilt

24 Blocks   4 across by 6 down
Finished size approx. 50" x 69" with borders

## TV Size

|  | Yardage to buy |  | Tear Strips selvage to selvage |  |
|---|---|---|---|---|
| Rail 1 and 3 | ⅔ yd. each |  | 6 strips  2 ½" wide |  |
| Wide 2nd Rail | 1 ¼ yds. |  | 6 strips  6" wide |  |
| 1st Border | ⅔ yd. |  | 6 strips  2 ½" wide |  |
| 2nd Border | 1 yd. |  | 7 strips  4" wide |  |
|  |  |  |  |  |
| Batting | 54" x 72" |  |  |  |
| Backing | 3 yds. |  |  |  |

## TV Size for using Picture Fabric

|  | Yardage to buy |  | Tear Strips |  |
|---|---|---|---|---|
| Rail 1 and 3 | ⅔ yd. each |  | 6 strips  2 ½" wide selvage to selvage |  |
| Wide 2nd Rail | 1 ⅞ yds. |  | 3 strips  6" wide selvage to selvage |  |
|  |  |  | and 3 strips  6" wide **ALONG THE SELVAGE** |  |
| 1st Border | ⅔ yd. |  | 6 strips  2 ½" wide selvage to selvage |  |
| 2nd Border | 1 yd. |  | 7 strips  4" wide selvage to selvage |  |
| Batting | 54" x 72" |  |  |  |
| Backing | 3 yds. |  |  |  |

# Twin Quilt

32 Blocks    4 across by 8 down
Finished size approx. 52" x 90" with 2 borders
*57" x 95" with 3rd border (optional)

## Twin Size

|  | Yardage to buy | | Tear Strips selvage to selvage | |
|---|---|---|---|---|
| Rail 1 and 3 | 1 yd. each | | 8 strips   2 ½" wide | |
| Wide 2nd Rail | 1 ⅔ yds. | | 8 strips   6" wide | |
| 1st Border | ⅞ yd. | | 7 strips   3" wide | |
| 2nd Border | 1 ⅔ yds. | | 9 strips   6" wide | |
| *3rd Border | 1 yd. | | 9 strips   3" wide | |
| Batting | 63" x 96" | | | |
| Backing | 5 ½ yds. or 1 ⅔ yds. of 96" wide fabric | | | |

## Twin Size for Using Picture Fabric

|  | Yardage to buy | | Tear Strips | |
|---|---|---|---|---|
| Rail 1 and 3 | 1 yd. each | | 8 strips   2 ½" wide selvage to selvage | |
| Wide 2nd Rail | 2 yds. | | 4 strips   6" wide selvage to selvage | |
|  | | | and 4 strips   6" wide **ALONG THE SELVAGE** | |
| 1st Border | ⅞ yd. | | 7 strips   3" wide selvage to selvage | |
| 2nd Border | 1 ⅔ yds. | | 9 strips   6" wide | |
| *3rd Border | 1 yd. | | 9 strips   3" wide | |
| Batting | 63" x 96" | | | |
| Backing | 5 ½ yds. or 1 ⅔ yds. of 96" wide fabric | | | |

# Sewing Tools You Need for Rail Fence

Sewing Machine

**Bonded batting**
A filling put inside the quilt that makes it fluffy and warm.

**6" x 12" Plastic Ruler**
This will help you measure correctly.

**Embroidery Floss**
Use 6 strands of the embroidery floss in a color that looks good with your quilt. You will use it in the curved needle to tie the quilt.

Quilting Pins

**Two Scissors**
Good sharp scissors to cut strip sets. Old paper scissors to cut paper, cardboard or plastic.

**Hand Sewing Needle**
Packaged needles that are used for hand sewing.

**Curved Needle for Tying**
This hook-shaped needle looks like a doctor's needle or an upholstery needle. Use it to catch the back of your quilt.

**Presser Foot**
The metal piece of the sewing machine that runs along the fabric.

**Magnetic Seam Guide**
This great tool helps you sew straight. Set it against the presser foot and run the edge of the fabric against it.

Neutral Thread

*Tip: Have someone grab every other clipped piece. You grab remaining clipped pieces. Now both of you pull. Presto!! Your strips are torn quickly and you had fun doing it.*

*Tip: If you are an experienced sewer you may use a rotary cutter instead of tearing.*

# Here We Go!

## Straightening 1st Rail Fabric

Cut a ½" long nick into the selvage side near one end of 1st Rail Fabric.

Hint: *A nick is a small cut. The selvage side is the edge of the fabric that doesn't stretch and doesn't have loose threads. Sometimes it has writing on it.*

Tear from that selvage side to the other selvage. This straightens the fabric.

　Repeat, Straightening Wide 2nd Rail Fabric

　Repeat, Straightening 3rd Rail Fabric

## Tearing the Narrow 1st and 3rd Rail Strips

1. Remove the Pattern Page from the book. Paste the whole page onto light-weight posterboard. Find the 2½" square. Cut on the line with paper scissors, not cloth scissors. This is called the 2½ " square template.

2. From the torn straight edge, use the template to measure 2½" along the selvage side. Draw a ½" long line.

3. Repeat drawing a line every 2½" for as many strips as you need of 1st and 3rd Rail Fabrics. Do not mark Wide 2nd Rail Fabric now.

| | |
|---|---|
| **Square Quilt** | **4 strips** |
| **TV Quilt** | **6 strips** |
| **Twin Quilt** | **8 strips** |

Making 2½" strips

4. Clip on the lines ½" through the selvage.

5. Tear the number of strips you need of each. Then fold in half and stack each pile.

# Tearing the Wide 2nd Rail Strip

1. Find the 6" square on the Pattern Page. Cut on the line with paper scissors, not cloth scissors. This is called the 6" square template.

2. From the torn straight edge, measure 6" along the selvage side. Draw a ½" long line. Follow the tearing chart carefully for picture fabric.

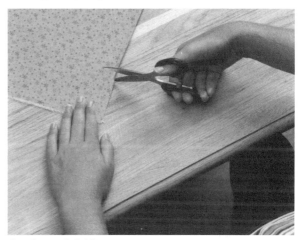
Cutting a "nick"

3. Repeat drawing a line every 6" for as many strips as you need of Wide 2nd Rail Fabric.

| | |
|---|---|
| **Square Quilt** | **4 strips** |
| **TV Quilt** | **6 strips** |
| **Twin Quilt** | **8 strips** |

4. Clip on the lines ½" long through the selvage.

5. Tear the number of strips you need. Fold in half and stack.

Tearing strips

# Ironing the Strips

1. After all strips are torn, iron the edges flat.

2. Clip any long loose threads.

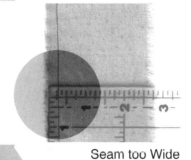
Seam too Wide

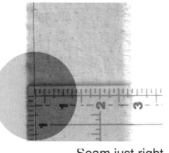
Seam just right

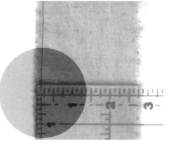
Seam too Narrow

# Hooray! Let's Sew

*All seam allowances will be ¼" wide. Place a magnetic seam guide along the right edge of the presser foot. The seam guide helps you sew a straight seam.*

In one inch, count your stitches. Are there 12? 15?

Use a small stitch such as 12 to 15 stitches per inch or #2.5 on some sewing machines.

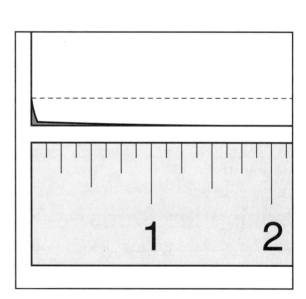

Lay out the strips of 1st and Wide 2nd Rail to the right of your machine like this:

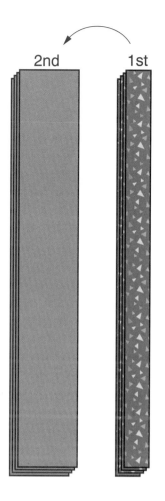

1. Flip 1st Rail onto Wide Rail, pretty sides together. The side of the fabric that shows the design best and is the brightest is called "the right side" or "the pretty side."

   Line up the top edges and the right side edges.

   You may need to pin the edges together.

   Put them under the presser foot with 1st Rail on the top.

*Hint: Hold the two edges together with your right hand about 6" from the sewing machine. Let your right hand ride with the fabric toward the needle until about 1" from the presser foot. Stop sewing. Put the edges together again and repeat.*

2. Sew down the right side of the 2 strips.

   **Keep the edges together**. Do not watch the needle of your machine. Keep the edges of your two strips together and just touching the seam guide.

   Sew as straight as possible. Stop if your edges aren't together.

   One strip may be longer than the other. *(That's okay!)*

   When you finish sewing these strips, cut the thread. Repeat sewing all your 1st Rail strips to all of your Wide Rail strips.

3. Open a sewn strip and lay it by a 3rd Rail strip.

Place the 3rd Rail on top of the wide strip, pretty sides together.

Line up the top edges, and sew lengthwise.

When you finish sewing these strips, cut the thread.

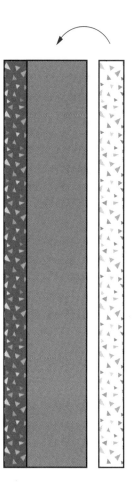

Repeat adding all your 3rd Rail strips to the sewn strips.

*This won't be hard, will it?*

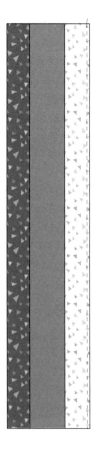

4.  Set the seam and iron  *(You what?!?)*

Lay the closed sewn strips on the ironing board with the narrow strips on top.

Iron on the stitching. This is "setting the seam."

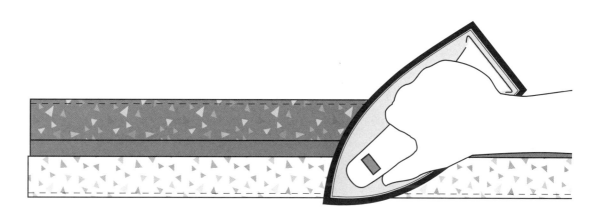

Open the narrow strips and iron from the center out to the edge.

 Make sure the set of strips is smooth and flat, and that the seam lines don't have folds or tucks. *(Oops! Get rid of those folds!)*

The seam allowances on the back should be ironed toward the narrow strips. This sewn strip is called a "strip set."

When you finish ironing this strip set, iron the other sewn strip sets.

You need this many strip sets:

| | |
|---|---|
| **Square Quilt** | 4 |
| **TV Quilt** | 6 |
| **Twin Quilt** | 8 |

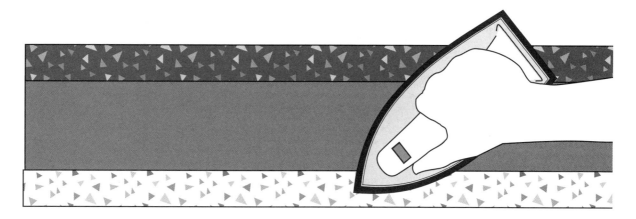

# Cutting the Blocks

 ## Cutting the Strip Set *(This is scary)*

1. Lay the edge of the strip set along the table edge to keep the strips straight. Measure across the strip set from edge to edge.

   It will be about 10" wide.

2. Draw a circle around the number closest to your measurement:

   9 ¼"          9 ½"          9 ¾"          10"

Measure at both ends and in the middle for an average measurement

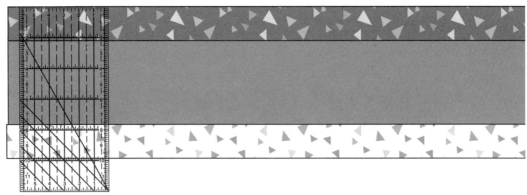

3. From the Pattern Page, find the large square which is the measurement size you circled.

4. Carefully cut out the square with paper scissors, not your cloth scissors.

   Be very accurate.

   This is a template.

5. Measure your template across and down.

   It should be the same size as your circled measurement.

6. Lay the strip set along the edge of the table.

7. Lay your template even with the edge of your fabric and near the end of the strip set.

8. Hold the template firmly and draw a pencil line against both sides of the template. The pencil lead must be sharp. Use a colored pencil that shows on your fabric.

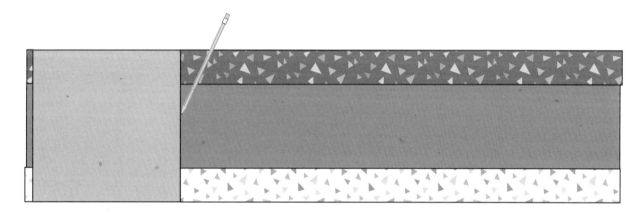

9. Carefully cut on the first pencil line to remove the selvages and get a straight end on the strip set. Then cut on the second line to make your first Rail Fence square block.

10. From the straight cut edge, continue to mark the rest of the strip set.

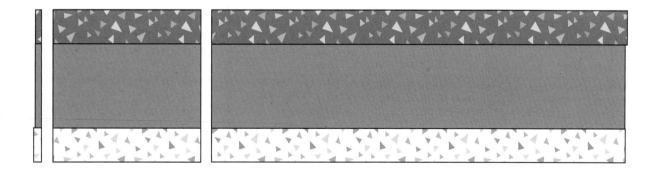

11. Carefully and accurately cut on each drawn line.  You should get 4 blocks from each strip set. You will have very little left over so be careful.

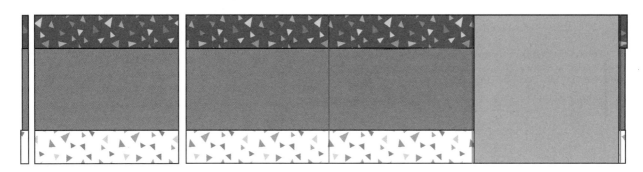

You need this many Rail Fence  blocks:

**Square Quilt**         16

**TV Quilt**              24

**Twin Quilt**           32

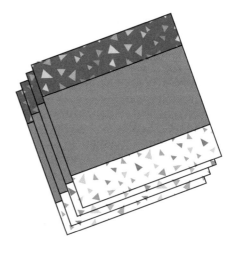

─── 10" square ───

─── 9 ¼" square ───
─── 9 ½" square ───
─── 9 ¾" square ───
─── 10" square ───

# Rail Fence Pattern Page

Remove the Pattern Page from the book.
Paste the whole page onto lightweight posterboard.

2½" square

6" square

# Sewing the Blocks Together

Windmill Layout

Split Rail Layout

There are two different ways to lay out your blocks.  Choose your favorite.

## Example of
## Windmill Layout

## Example of
## Split Rail

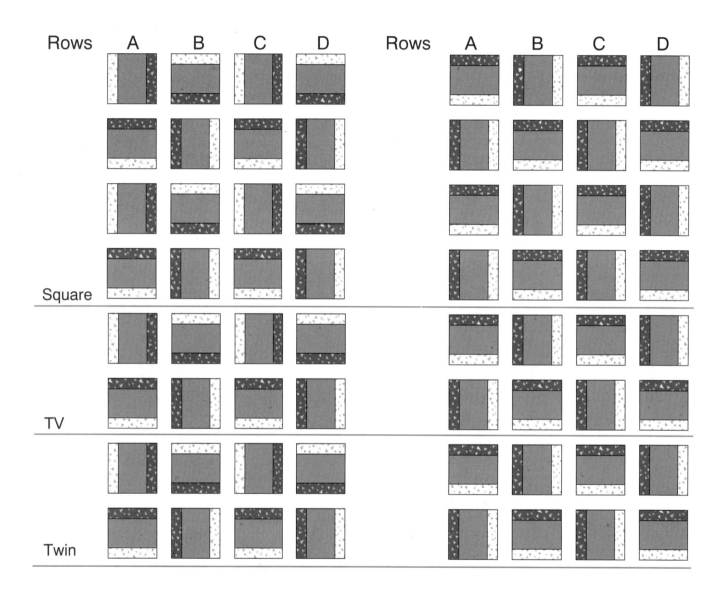

# Ready to Sew the Blocks Together *(Yeah!)*

## Sewing Row A and Row B

Pictures are examples of the TV Size Quilt using the Split Rail layout.

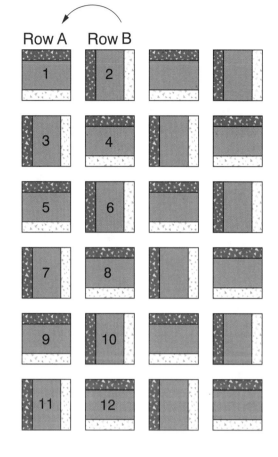

1. Flip Row B blocks on top of Row A blocks right (pretty) sides together.

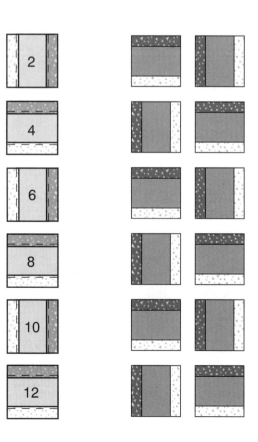

2. Pin the top and bottom of each pair of blocks on the right edge. Stretch the blocks if you need to make the edges meet.

3. Starting at the top of Rows A/B, pick up the blocks and stack in a pile.

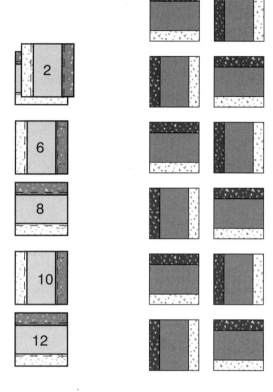

The number "2" block will always be on top.

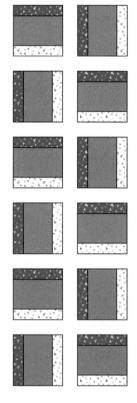

4. Sew Block 1 and Block 2 down the right side where you have pinned. Keep all the edges together and even.

   Sew slowly over the pins or take them out.

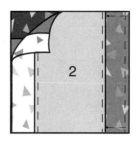

5. Butt and sew Block 3 and Block 4 next.

   Butt means place one block just touching another block.

6. Repeat butting and sewing the blocks together until you reach the bottom of the row for your size quilt.

   The blocks will be hooked together.

   **Do Not clip apart.**

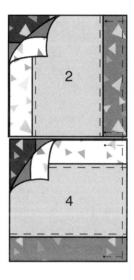

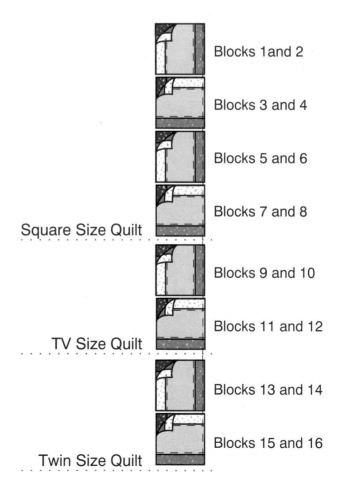

Blocks 1 and 2

Blocks 3 and 4

Blocks 5 and 6

Blocks 7 and 8

Square Size Quilt

Blocks 9 and 10

Blocks 11 and 12

TV Size Quilt

Blocks 13 and 14

Blocks 15 and 16

Twin Size Quilt

7. Open Blocks 1 and 2 pretty side showing. Open Blocks 3 and 4 pretty side showing.

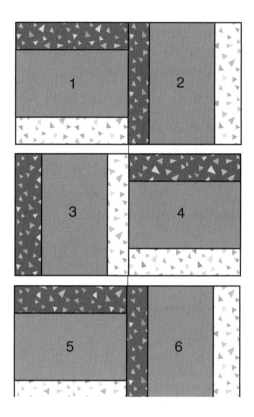

8. Fold Blocks 1 and 2 down on top of Blocks 3 and 4 pretty sides together.

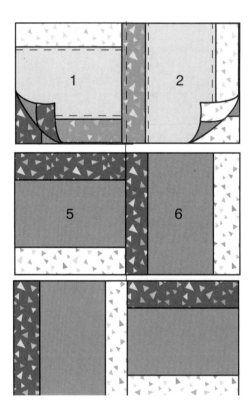

9.  Match the seams by pushing one up and the other down.  Pin and sew across the two blocks.

Sew

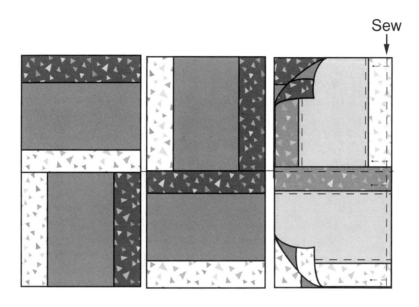

10. Repeat sewing seams on the the blocks until Row A and Row B are sewn together both down and across.

Sew

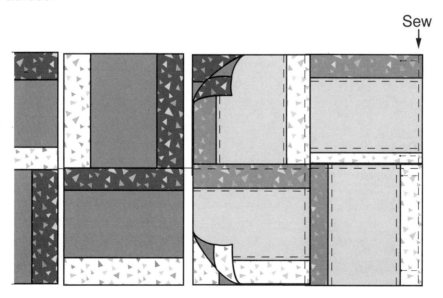

# Sewing Row C and Row D

1. Place Row D blocks on top of Row C blocks pretty sides together.

2. Repeat butting and sewing blocks for Rows C and D as you did for Rows A and B.

3. Open blocks and sew across just as before.

   You now have two sets of sewn rows.

*Yippy, Skippy! It's beginning to look like a quilt!*

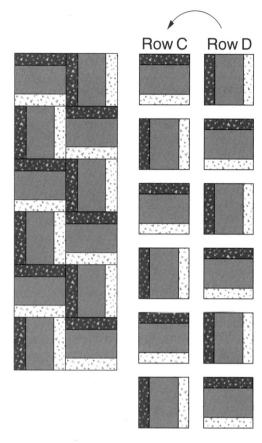

Row C   Row D

4. Lay out the 2 sets of sewn rows.

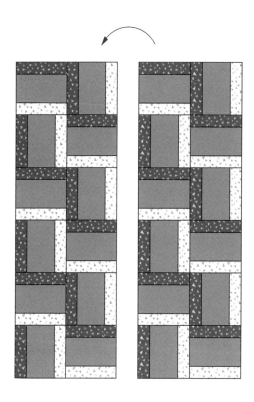

5. Lay one set on the other, pretty sides together, and sew the middle seam. Make the seams meet by pinning them together. Sew all the way to the bottom.

6. When all your blocks are sewn together, it is called a "quilt top."

7. Iron your quilt top.

*Guess what!  You did it!*

**Jump and Shout!**

*Your quilt top is together!!*

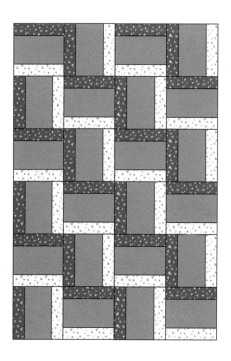

*Borders make your quilt look great. Borders are strips sewn around the whole quilt top to frame it.*

# Borders

1. Straighten the Border Fabric by clipping and tearing as you did when you started tearing strips.

2. Look at your tearing chart on page12, 13 or 14 to find how many border strips you need.

   The chart will also tell you how wide the border strips should be.

3. Tear the number of strips you need.

4. Press each border strip from selvage to selvage.

5. Lay your ruler just covering a selvage end of a strip.

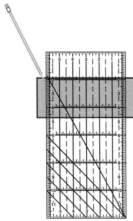

6. Draw a line along the edge of the ruler.

7. Cut on the drawn line to remove the selvage and have a straight end.

8. Repeat removing the selvage and straightening each end of each border strip.

# Sewing borders to the quilt *(This will be easy.)*

Lay your quilt out flat, pretty side up. *(Looks great doesn't it?)*

1. Lay one of the short border strips on the top edge of your quilt, pretty sides together.

2. Smooth the strip with your hands and pin about every 4 or 5 inches across the top.

3. With your scissors clip the border at the quilt edge. Tear across the border so it is even with the edge of the quilt.

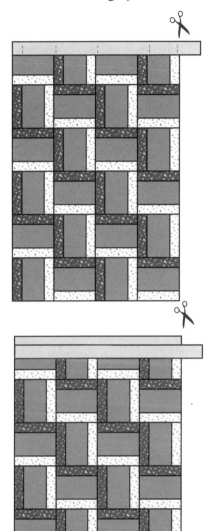

4. Lay the other short border strip on top of the one you just pinned.

5. With your scissors clip and tear your border at the edge of the quilt. Both borders should be the same length. *(Oh, I hope so, or you will have a crooked quilt!)*

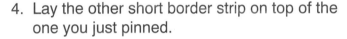
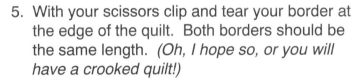

6. Pin this measured strip to the bottom of the quilt, pretty sides together. Pin at each end of the strip. Then pin in the middle. Now pin every 4 or 5 inches.

   You may need to stretch the quilt or the border to make the ends meet.

7. Sew the top and bottom border strips to the quilt. Keep the edges even and together. Be careful when you come to the pins. You can sew slowly over the pins or pull them out.

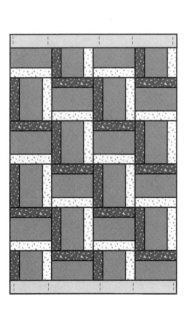

8. After you've sewn on the top and bottom borders and have taken the pins out, set the seam by ironing on the stitching.

9. Iron the border out flat. All seams on the borders should iron toward the border strips and away from the quilt blocks.

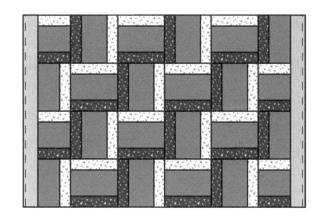

10. Iron away any folds or tucks along the seam lines.

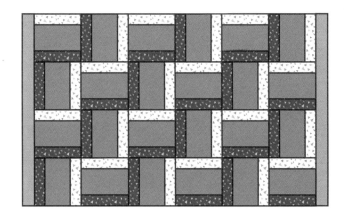

11. Sew the rest of the First Border strips pretty sides together across the short ends into one long strip.

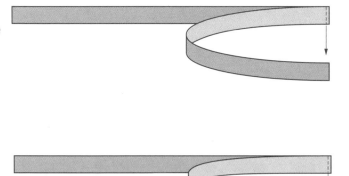

12. Lay the long first border strip along the side edge of the quilt from border edge to border edge, pretty sides together. *(What, again?)*

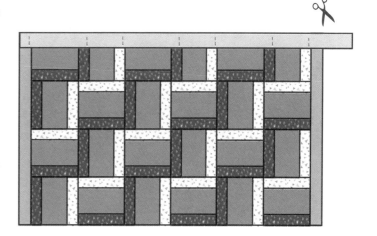

13. Smooth and pin the border to the quilt. Clip and tear off the extra.

14. Lay the rest of the border strip on the top of the one you just pinned. Clip and tear at the quilt edge. Both borders should be the same length.

15. Pin the border strip to the last side making the border fit the quilt.

16. Sew the border strips to the quilt. Border edges should be even and together. *(Does this sound familiar!)*

17. Set the seam by ironing on the stitching.

18. Iron the borders out flat with the seam ironed toward the border.

19. For the TV and Twin Size quilts, sew all your Second Border strips into one long strip.

20. Measure, pin and sew them on to the top and bottom like you did with the First Border. *(Gee, you do it each time!!)*

21. Repeat for the two sides of the quilt. *(Again!)*

Your quilt top is finished when you have all the borders on it. The Square Size quilt has one border. The TV Size has two borders. The Twin Size can have two or three borders.

*You are in the home stretch. Your quilt is almost finished. Wow! This quilt looks awesome.*

# Sewing the Backing Pieces Together

## Sewing the Backing Pieces Together

1. Measure across your quilt.

2. Measure down the selvage of the backing fabric that measurement plus 3" and draw a ½" long line.

3. Clip the selvage on the line. Tear the fabric across from selvage to selvage.

4. Tear another piece of backing fabric exactly the same measurement.

5. Clip and tear the selvage off of the two backing fabrics.

6. Pin the two backing fabrics pretty sides together.

7. Sew down the right edge of the backing fabrics.

8. Press seam to one side.

   Your backing is now ready for the quilt top!

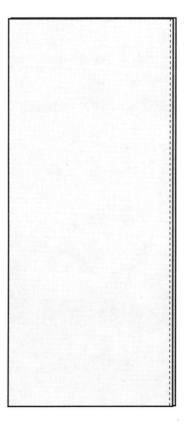

# Finishing
# Your Quilt

## Finishing Your Quilt with a Quick Turn

*(Is this a Magic Trick?)*

**How exciting!  We are about to finish the quilt.**

This is a simple way to finish a quilt.  It is fast and easy.

1. Place the backing for the quilt, pretty side up, on a flat surface.

2. Make sure it is smooth, but do not pull tight.

3. Tape the edges of the backing to the flat surface with masking tape.

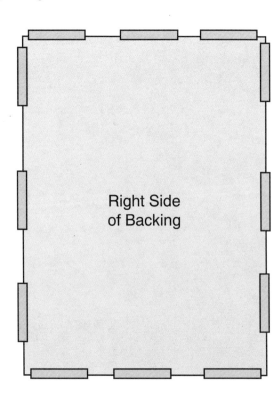

Right Side
of Backing

4. Lay the quilt top on the smoothed backing, pretty side down, wrong side up.

5. Pin the quilt top to the backing about every 4" to 5" all around, leaving 16" unpinned along one side. This part is not sewn.

*Hint: Put two pins at the beginning and end of the 16" so you will know where to start and stop sewing.*

6. Take off the tape. Carry your quilt to your machine. *Get ready to sew.*

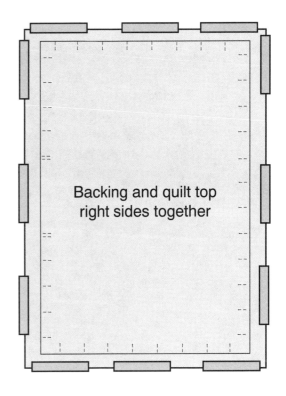

Backing and quilt top
right sides together

7. Sew around the outside edges with a ¼" seam, leaving the 16" unsewn.

8. Cut off the extra backing so the quilt top and backing edges are even.

9. Lay the batting out on a flat surface.

10. Place the quilt on top of the batting with the wrong side of the blocks showing. The batting should be big enough to show around the edges.

   Smooth well.

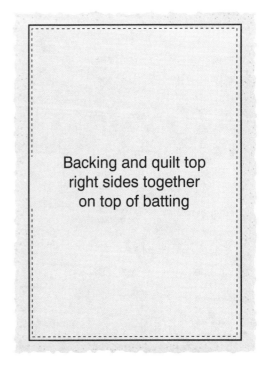

Backing and quilt top
right sides together
on top of batting

11. Thread a large hand sewing needle with about 22" inches of sewing thread. Knot the end of a single thread. With a large basting or running stitch, hand sew the quilt to the batting along the very edge of the quilt. Don't baste across the 16" not pinned.

**Do not baste into the stitched seam.**

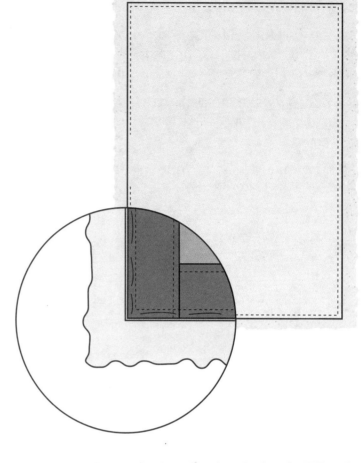

12. Cut off the batting so all edges are even.

# Now for the fun!  This is called "Birthing a Quilt."

It will be easier if there are 2 or 3 of you to roll the quilt.  Get a couple of friends to help you.

1. Roll the quilt and batting from the corners toward the opening.

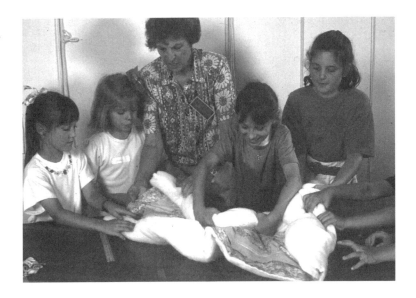

2. Reach through the opening and start to pull the quilt right side out.

3. Pull the quilt through the opening. (This is really cool!)

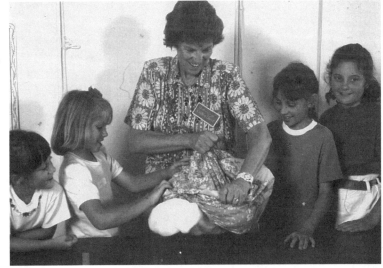

4. Unroll the quilt carefully.  It is now pretty side out.

5. Pull the quilt and shake until it is smooth.

6. Pull out the corners.  You may need a needle to pull the corners out full.

7. At the quilt opening push the two edges of the fabric to the inside. Pin the quilt opening closed.

   With a needle and thread, hand sew the opening of the quilt closed.

8. Pin the center of each block with a straight pin. Be sure the pin goes through to the back. This will hold the quilt top, batting and back together until you get it tied.

9. Thread a large or curved needle with 6 strands of embroidery thread about 20 inches long.

10. Start at a block in the corner of the quilt and take a stitch through all layers—quilt top, batting and backing.

11. Pull the thread through all layers then go to the center of the next block.

   **The thread will be one long piece, do not cut**

12. Keep sewing from corner to center to corner of the blocks until you are out of thread. Then thread your needle again.

   Put some tie stitches in the borders, too.

13. Cut the thread between the stitches.

14. Tie the threads with a square knot. *(What kind of knot?)*

15. Take the thread on the right and wrap it two times around the left thread.

16. Pull the knot tight.

17. Take the thread on the left, wrap it two times around the thread on the right. *(Tricky, isn't it?)*

18. Pull the knot tight.

19. Clip the threads the length you like...about ½" to 1" long.

## Guess What

*Your Rail Fence Quilt is finished!*

*Three cheers and a pat on the back you did a great job*

*Show your quilt off to everyone!*

*Start taking orders.  Everyone will want a quilt just like yours.*

# Ideas to make Your Rail Fence Different

1. Make the wide rails of half of the blocks one color, and make the wide rails of the rest of the blocks another color.

2. Draw around your hand with a crayon on the plain wide rail. Place a cloth over the crayon and iron it to make the color stay on the fabric.

3. Copies of photographs can be put in the plain wide rail with a product you can buy called "Picture This."

4. For half of your blocks put 1st Rail fabric on both sides of the Wide 2nd Rail. On the other half of your blocks put 3rd Rail fabric on both sides of the Wide 2nd Rail. When the blocks are put together this looks like a basket weave.

5. Jessica used three narrow rail fabrics to create an original third rail running through the quilt.

6. You can draw pictures or write the names of your friends on plain wide rails. Use special pens for writing on fabric.

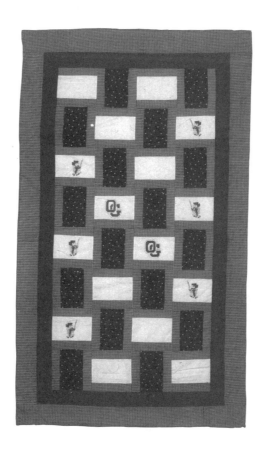

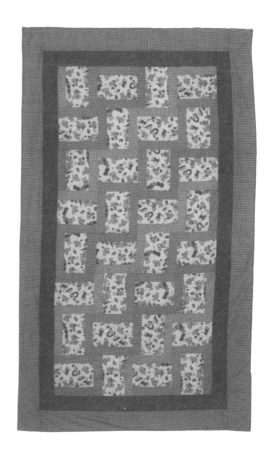

# Order Information

If you do not have a quilt shop in your area, you may write for a complete catalog and current price list of all books and patterns published by Quilt in a Day®, Inc.

## Books

Quilt in a Day Log Cabin
The Sampler—A Machine Sewn Quilt
Trio of Treasured Quilts
Lover's Knot Quilt
Amish Quilt in a Day
Irish Chain in a Day
Country Christmas
May Basket Quilt
Diamond Log Cabin Tablecloth or Treeskirt
Morning Star Quilt
Trip Around the World Quilt
Dresden Plate Quilt, A Simplified Method
Pineapple Quilt, a Piece of Cake
Radiant Star Quilt
Blazing Star Tablecloth
Tulip Quilt
Scrap Quilt, Strips and Spider Webs
Burgoyne Surrounded
Sunbonnet Sue Visits Quilt in a Day
Creating With Color
Christmas Quilts and Crafts
Quilter's Year
Baskets & Flowers
Quilters Almanac
Christmas Traditions
Stars Across America
Kaleidoscope
Machine Quilting Primer
Jewel Box Quilt
Nana's Garden

## Booklets and Patterns

Patchwork Santa
Last Minute Gifts
Angel of Antiquity
Log Cabin Wreath Wallhanging
Log Cabin Christmas Tree Wallhanging
Flying Geese Quilt
Miniature May Basket Wallhanging
Tulip Table Runner and Wallhanging
Heart's Delight, Nine-Patch Variations
Country Flag Wallhanging
Spools and Tools Wallhanging
Schoolhouse Wallhanging
Star for all Seasons

## Videos

Log Cabin Video
Lover's Knot Video
Irish Chain Video
Ohio Star Video
Blazing Star Video
Scrap Quilt Video
Morning Star Video
Trip Around the World Video
Pineapple Video
Radiant Star Video
Flying Geese Video
and many others

If you are ever in San Diego County, southern California, drop by the Quilt in a Day center quilt shop and classroom in the La Costa Meadows Industrial Park. Write ahead for a current class schedule and map. Eleanor Burns may be seen on Public Broadcasting Stations (PBS) throughout the country. Check TV listings in your area.

Quilt in a Day, Inc.
1955 Diamond Street, San Marcos, California 92069-5122
www.quilt-in-a-day.com • e-mail: qiad@quilt-in-a-day.com
Orders: 800 777-4852 Information Line: 760 591-0929 fax: 760 591-4424